It is as tragic as it is common for Christians to think the doctrine of the Trinity is irrelevant to everyday life. Liz McQuoid's studies do a sterling job of showing us how vital and practical it is to understand the Trinity. This wonderful set of studies will be a feast for individuals and Bible study groups.
Sam Allberry, Associate Minister at St Mary's Church, Maidenhead, and author of Connected: Living in the Light of the Trinity, *and* Lifted: Experiencing the Resurrection Life

The truth and reality of the Trinity lie at the heart of our faith, life and worship as Christians. This set of Bible studies will help you explore this wonderful theme, engaging your heart, stretching your mind and changing your life!
Dr Steve Brady, Principal, Moorlands College, Christchurch

The idea of one God who exists in community as three persons is not an easy one to grasp. There are no straightforward 'proof texts' in the Bible that sum it up for us. This study guide seeks to aid our understanding of this key Christian concept. It will encourage you to dig deep into Scripture and to consider the personal impact of being caught up into this divine community of Father, Son and Holy Spirit.
Elaine Duncan, Chief Executive of Scottish Bible Society

The Transforming Trinity

Rediscovering the heart of our faith

7 Studies for Individuals
or Small Groups

Elizabeth McQuoid

INTER-VARSITY PRESS
Norton Street, Nottingham NG7 3HR, England
Email: ivp@ivpbooks.com
Website: www.ivpbooks.com

First published 2013

British Library Cataloguing in Publication Data
A catalogue record for this book is available from the British Library.

ISBN: 978–1–84474–906–5

Set in Warnock
Typeset in Great Britain by CRB Associates, Potterhanworth, Lincolnshire
Printed and bound in Great Britain by Ashford Colour Press Ltd, Gosport, Hampshire

Inter-Varsity Press publishes Christian books that are true to the Bible and that communicate the gospel, develop discipleship and strengthen the church for its mission in the world.

Inter-Varsity Press is closely linked with the Universities and Colleges Christian Fellowship, a student movement connecting Christian Unions in universities and colleges throughout Great Britain, and a member movement of the International Fellowship of Evangelical Students. Website: www.uccf.org.uk

Contents

Introduction

The word *Trinity* is never mentioned in the Bible. And yet evidence for one God in three persons is found throughout the Scriptures. When the Israelites fled from Egypt, Moses taught them about the uniqueness and unity of God – 'Hear O Israel: The LORD our God, the LORD is one' (Deuteronomy 6:4). This vital message was to ground their faith and be passed on to their children. And as the storyline of the Bible unfolds, the different persons of the Trinity – Father, Son and Holy Spirit – are revealed, each with different roles but one in essence and purpose.

As Christians we *say* we believe in the doctrine of the Trinity but in practice we often ignore it. For many of us this exclusive claim of Christianity has become irrelevant and unimportant, a topic reserved for theologians. So, unintentionally, we focus on one person of the Trinity, excluding the others. We fall into the trap of seeing the Father as the God of the Old Testament and Jesus as the God of the New. We make a distinction between Word and Spirit, assuming it's OK for some Christians to be open to the Spirit while others rely on the Word.

We need to rediscover the Trinity because 'in the confession of the Trinity throbs the heart of the Christian religion' (Bavinck, *Doctrine of God*, p. 281). In this study we will find out why the Trinity is central to our beliefs and fundamental to the working out of our faith. We will never exhaust the riches of the Trinity – it is a mystery. But as we grow in our understanding of God we will learn to worship him more fully, reflect his image more clearly and experience his transforming power in our lives.

STUDY INTRODUCTIONS

To help participants get the most out of these studies, there is a free supplement, available by email, ebook and in other formats, that introduces the subject of each study. This includes the passage to be studied and an introductory question designed to help anyone begin to think about the subject of each study and how it affects them. It is also designed to be accessible to those who don't have much time to sit down and prepare. These will enrich your study time, and help you get into the right frame of mind. You can register yourself or group members at www.ivpbooks.com/transformingtrinity

SESSION 1

Saved by the triune God

▶ INTRODUCTION

The Trinity is not some obscure theological doctrine to debate. It is at the heart of our salvation. The work of the Trinity at the cross confounds the idea that God is distant, unconcerned with humanity; it rejects the notion that the Son was an unwilling victim or an independent operator. Our salvation was so precious to God that each member of the Trinity was involved. And it is at the cross that the Trinity displayed itself most gloriously.

READ *Ephesians 1:3–14*

> ³*Praise be to the God and Father of our Lord Jesus Christ, who has blessed us in the heavenly realms with every spiritual blessing in Christ.* ⁴*For he chose us in him before the creation of the world to be holy and blameless in his sight. In love* ⁵*he predestined us for adoption to sonship through Jesus Christ, in accordance with his pleasure and will –* ⁶*to the praise of his glorious grace, which he has freely given us in the One he loves.* ⁷*In him we have redemption through his blood, the forgiveness of sins, in accordance with the riches of God's grace* ⁸*that he lavished on us. With all wisdom and understanding,* ⁹*he made known to us the mystery of his will according to his good pleasure, which he purposed in Christ,* ¹⁰*to be put into effect when the times reach their fulfilment – to bring unity to all things in heaven and on earth under Christ.*
>
> ¹¹*In him we were also chosen, having been predestined according to the plan of him who works out everything in conformity with the purpose of his will,* ¹²*in order that we, who were the first to put our hope in Christ, might be for the praise of his glory.* ¹³*And you also were included in Christ when you heard the message of truth, the gospel of your salvation. When you believed, you were marked in him with a seal, the promised Holy Spirit,* ¹⁴*who is a deposit guaranteeing our inheritance until the redemption of those who are God's possession – to the praise of his glory.*

 FOCUS ON THE THEME

1. Why do you think we don't talk much about the Trinity today?

🔍 WHAT DOES THE BIBLE SAY?

2. What do these verses tell us about the different roles of the Father, Son and Holy Spirit in our salvation?

3. What do we learn about the Father's character from these verses?

4. The Father, Son and Holy Spirit have different roles in salvation, but what is their common purpose?

It is especially when we reflect on the relation of the three persons to the divine essence that all analogies fail us and we become deeply conscious of the fact that the Trinity is a mystery far beyond our comprehension. It is the incomprehensible glory of the Godhead. (Berkhof, *Systematic Theology*, p. 88)

◎ INVESTIGATE FURTHER

5. Look at Mark 1:1–15. What are the different functions of the members of the Trinity in these verses?

6a. Why is it crucial for our salvation that Jesus was fully God? Look at Hebrews 7:23–27.

b. Why is it crucial for our salvation that Jesus was fully human? Look at Hebrews 2:14–18.

7. What does Philippians 2:6–11 tell us about Jesus' role in the Trinity?

❤️ LIVING IT OUT

8. According to 2 Corinthians 1:21–22, how does the Trinity help us persevere as Christians?

9. You are talking to a friend who says he doesn't believe in God. But the God he describes is impersonal and unconcerned with human suffering. What would you say to him?

10. We often feel guilty about our sin and wonder whether there are some sins God can't forgive. What does the work of the Trinity at the cross say to us?

 PRAYER TIME

Ephesians 1:3–14 begins and ends with praise to God. Spend some time praising Father, Son and Holy Spirit for all that they did to save you. Next pray for those you know who are struggling in their faith. Ask the triune God to strengthen them and help them persevere. Finally pray for your loved ones who are not Christians. Ask the Holy Spirit to work in their lives so that they would know God's love and accept Jesus' sacrifice for them on the cross.

 FURTHER STUDY

What does Colossians 1:1–23 teach us about the persons of the Trinity, their roles and how they operate in our lives?

SESSION 2

Knowing the Father

▶ INTRODUCTION

Because God calls himself 'Father' we tend to view him through the lens of our own experience of fatherhood – whether good or bad. We forget that even the best earthly father cannot compare to God as our Father. In fact our premise is all wrong; it's not our earthly parents who should shape our understanding of God, but God who must shape our thinking about what it means to be a father. We need to study the Scriptures to find the truth about God and to grasp the assurance, freedom and joy of knowing him as Father.

READ *Galatians 3:23 - 4:7*

[23] *Before the coming of this faith, we were held in custody under the law, locked up until the faith that was to come would be revealed.* [24] *So the law was our guardian until Christ came that we might be justified by faith.* [25] *Now that this faith has come, we are no longer under a guardian.*

[26] *So in Christ Jesus you are all children of God through faith,* [27] *for all of you who were baptised into Christ have clothed yourselves with Christ.* [28] *There is neither Jew nor Gentile, neither slave nor free, nor is there male and female, for you are all one in Christ Jesus.* [29] *If you belong to Christ, then you are Abraham's seed, and heirs according to the promise.*

[1] *What I am saying is that as long as an heir is under age, he is no different from a slave, although he owns the whole estate.* [2] *The heir is subject to guardians and trustees until the time set by his father.* [3] *So also, when we were under age, we were in slavery under the elemental spiritual forces of the world.* [4] *But when the set time had fully come, God sent his Son, born of a woman, born under the law,* [5] *to redeem those under the law, that we might receive adoption to sonship.* [6] *Because you are his sons, God sent the Spirit of his Son into our hearts, the Spirit who calls out, 'Abba, Father.'* [7] *So you are no longer a slave, but God's child; and since you are his child, God has made you also an heir.*

 FOCUS ON THE THEME

1. Do you struggle with the concept of God as Father?

 WHAT DOES THE BIBLE SAY?

2. How do we become sons and daughters of God? In Galatians 3:26–29 what phrases are used to describe our relationship to Christ? What does each of them mean?

3. How do we know we are truly heirs of God? What is the guarantee of our sonship? Look at verses 4–7.

This resurrection life you received from God is not a timid, grave-tending life. It's adventurously expectant, greeting God with a childlike 'What's next, Papa?' God's Spirit touches our spirits and confirms who we really are. We know who he is, and we know who we are: Father and children. And we know we are going to get what's coming to us – an unbelievable inheritance!   (Romans 8:15–16 MSG)

◎ INVESTIGATE FURTHER

4. We are now sons and daughters of God, but in what sense are we still slaves? Look at Romans 6:15–18.

5.   What do Matthew 7:7–11 and Ephesians 3:14 teach us about how we approach God as Father?

6.   What difference should being a child of God make to how we live? Look at 1 John 2:28 – 3:10.

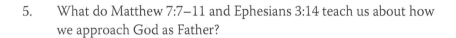 LIVING IT OUT

7.   How can remembering you're a child of God help you through difficulties in life?

8.   It is often hard to pray. How does knowing God as Father help?

9.   In the light of this study do you need to alter your perception of God as Father?

▲ PRAYER TIME

Imagine the scene in Matthew 7:7–11. Come to your *Abba* Father. Ask . . . seek . . . knock . . . Pray for one another today and throughout the week. Bring before God your deepest concerns and troubles. Rest assured that your heavenly Father hears your prayers and he will give you what is best.

● FURTHER STUDY

What role does each member of the Trinity play in our prayers? Look at John 16:23–24; Romans 8:26–27; Ephesians 2:18.

SESSION 3

Following the Son

▶ INTRODUCTION

The members of the Trinity are equally and fully divine but each has a different role within the Godhead. Jesus' role as the incarnate Son was to obey the will of God the Father. Essentially this meant carrying out on earth the plans the Trinity had conceived in heaven. When we become children of God we join Jesus in his mission to do the Father's will. Following Christ involves us knowing him personally, studying and obeying God's Word, and serving him in the power of the Holy Spirit. In essence, following Jesus means learning to be like him: wholehearted in our devotion and submission to the Father.

READ *Mark 10:17-31*

[17]*As Jesus started on his way, a man ran up to him and fell on his knees before him. 'Good teacher,' he asked, 'what must I do to inherit eternal life?'*

[18]*'Why do you call me good?' Jesus answered. 'No one is good – except God alone.* [19]*You know the commandments: "You shall not murder, you shall not commit adultery, you shall not steal, you shall not give false testimony, you shall not defraud, honour your father and mother."'*

[20]*'Teacher,' he declared, 'all these I have kept since I was a boy.'*

[21]*Jesus looked at him and loved him. 'One thing you lack,' he said. 'Go, sell everything you have and give to the poor, and you will have treasure in heaven. Then come, follow me.'*

[22]*At this the man's face fell. He went away sad, because he had great wealth.*

[23]*Jesus looked round and said to his disciples, 'How hard it is for the rich to enter the kingdom of God!'*

[24]*The disciples were amazed at his words. But Jesus said again, 'Children, how hard it is to enter the kingdom of God!* [25]*It is easier for a camel to go through the eye of a needle than for someone who is rich to enter the kingdom of God.'*

[26]*The disciples were even more amazed, and said to each other, 'Who then can be saved?'*

[27]*Jesus looked at them and said, 'With man this is impossible, but not with God; all things are possible with God.'*

[28]*Then Peter spoke up, 'We have left everything to follow you!'*

[29]*'Truly I tell you,' Jesus replied, 'no one who has left home or brothers or sisters or mother or father or children or fields for me and the gospel* [30]*will fail to receive a hundred times as much in this present age: homes, brothers, sisters, mothers, children and fields – along with persecutions – and in the age to come eternal life.* [31]*But many who are first will be last, and the last first.'*

◐ FOCUS ON THE THEME

1. Imagine a court is trying to convict you for being a Christian. What evidence would it find that you are a follower of Christ?

◯ WHAT DOES THE BIBLE SAY?

2. How was the man trying to get into heaven? What was wrong with his efforts?

3. Giving all we have to the poor doesn't save us, so what is Jesus teaching in this passage?

4. Look at the context. When Jesus said, 'With man this is impossible, but not with God' (v. 27), what was he meaning?

5. What does Jesus promise for those who follow him wholeheartedly?

⊙ INVESTIGATE FURTHER

6. Look at Deuteronomy 6:4–5 and Mark 12:29–30. When God refers to his oneness or unity, what does he also say about our devotion?

7. When we follow Jesus, in what ways are we also imitating him? Look at Matthew 26:39; John 6:38; 17:4; Hebrews 10:5–7.

♥ LIVING IT OUT

8. What areas of life do we have trouble surrendering to Jesus? Why do we hold back from giving him our all?

9. It's easy to compartmentalize life – having a sacred/secular divide where some parts of life belong to God, but the rest belongs to us. In what ways are you tempted to do this?

    • Do you behave one way with your Christian friends and another with work colleagues?

    • Is 'church' a community or somewhere you go on Sunday?

- Do you spend money like it's yours or God's?

- Are you keen to obey all of God's commands or just the ones you like?

10. How can we make our devotion to God more wholehearted and less compartmentalized?

▲ PRAYER TIME

Bring to God areas of your life, people, situations you have not submitted to him or that you need to resubmit. For each issue say to God: 'Yet not as I will, but as you will' (Matthew 26:39).

If you are not already in a prayer triplet or an accountability group, then it might be good to find another believer you could pray with regularly. Meet together to pray, read Scripture, perhaps discuss a Christian book you are both reading. Encourage each other to follow Jesus wholeheartedly, copying his obedience and submission to God.

● FURTHER STUDY

What should motivate or spur us on to follow Christ wholeheartedly? Look at Ephesians 2:1–10.

Walking in the Spirit

▶ INTRODUCTION

The Holy Spirit is not a mystical force at home on the set of *Star Wars*. He is a divine person, a member of the Trinity. From Genesis 1:2 and throughout the Old and New Testaments we see him at work – revealing God to people, convicting, empowering and guiding into truth. At Jesus' baptism the Trinity works together and the Spirit anoints Jesus for ministry (Mark 1:9–13). After opening our hearts to salvation, the Holy Spirit does the same for us: the ever-present God-with-us helps us grow in holiness and equips us for service. Are you ignoring him, expecting sporadic but spectacular input from him or are you learning to walk with him every day?

READ *Romans 8:1-17*

¹*Therefore, there is now no condemnation for those who are in Christ Jesus,* ²*because through Christ Jesus the law of the Spirit who gives life has set you free from the law of sin and death.* ³*For what the law was powerless to do because it was weakened by the flesh, God did by sending his own Son in the likeness of sinful flesh to be a sin offering. And so he condemned sin in the flesh,* ⁴*in order that the righteous requirement of the law might be fully met in us, who do not live according to the flesh but according to the Spirit.*

⁵*Those who live according to the flesh have their minds set on what the flesh desires; but those who live in accordance with the Spirit have their minds set on what the Spirit desires.* ⁶*The mind governed by the flesh is death, but the mind governed by the Spirit is life and peace.* ⁷*The mind governed by the flesh is hostile to God; it does not submit to God's law, nor can it do so.* ⁸*Those who are in the realm of the flesh cannot please God.*

⁹*You, however, are not in the realm of the flesh but are in the realm of the Spirit, if indeed the Spirit of God lives in you. And if anyone does not have the Spirit of Christ, they do not belong to Christ.* ¹⁰*But if Christ is in you, then even though your body is subject to death because of sin, the Spirit gives life because of righteousness.* ¹¹*And if the Spirit of him who raised Jesus from the dead is living in you, he who raised Christ from the dead will also give life to your mortal bodies because of his Spirit who lives in you.*

¹²*Therefore, brothers and sisters, we have an obligation – but it is not to the flesh, to live according to it.* ¹³*For if you live according to the flesh, you will die; but if by the Spirit you put to death the misdeeds of the body, you will live.*

¹⁴*For those who are led by the Spirit of God are the children of God.* ¹⁵*The Spirit you received does not make you slaves, so that you live in fear again; rather, the Spirit you received brought about your adoption to sonship. And by him we cry, 'Abba, Father.'* ¹⁶*The Spirit himself testifies with our spirit that we are God's children.* ¹⁷*Now if we are children, then we are heirs – heirs of God and co-heirs with Christ, if indeed we share in his sufferings in order that we may also share in his glory.*

 FOCUS ON THE THEME

1. What images does the Bible use to describe the Holy Spirit? How do they help us understand him?

WHAT DOES THE BIBLE SAY?

2. Describe the two types of people mentioned in the passage, particularly verses 5–9.

3. What, according to verses 11–16, is the Holy Spirit's role in the life of a believer?

4. According to Romans 8:13, is growing in holiness something we do or something the Spirit does in us?

⊙ INVESTIGATE FURTHER

5.   Look at Galatians 5:13–26. What is the evidence we are living by
        the Spirit?

6.   'If you are led by the Spirit, you are not under the law' (Galatians
        5:18). Is Paul saying we don't need to obey God's law? Are we free
        to do what we want?

7.   Galatians 5:25 says, 'Since we live by the Spirit, let us keep in step
        with the Spirit.' How do we make sure we keep in step with the
        Spirit and grow in holiness? Look at:

   • Psalm 1:1–2

   • Philippians 4:6–7

   • Hebrews 10:24–25

   • Hebrews 12:1

*Since this is the kind of life we have chosen, the life of the Spirit, let us make
sure that we do not just hold it as an idea in our heads or a sentiment in
our hearts, but work out its implications in every detail of our lives.*

(Galatians 5:25 MSG)

♥ LIVING IT OUT

8. What difference does it make to understand that the Holy Spirit is a person, a member of the Trinity, rather than an impersonal force?

9. What would you say to each of the following people?

    - A believer who feels trapped in a cycle of sin he can't stop

    - An apathetic Christian who says she lacks any desire to live according to the Spirit

    - A keen Christian making important decisions, anxious that he is walking 'in step with the Spirit'

10. What steps do you need to take to make sure you are not grieving the Holy Spirit but keeping in step with him and growing in holiness?

▲ PRAYER TIME

Spend some time in quiet. Visualize yourself walking in the Spirit – imagine the living God walking with you throughout all the joys and troubles of your day. Imagine God walking with you as you deal patiently with elderly parents, struggle with the demands of young children, spend time away from home with work, and try to resolve difficult church issues.

Are you allowing yourself to be led by the Holy Spirit – are you listening to the Spirit's prompting and serving in his power – or are you running ahead with your agenda and priorities? Pray for one another that daily you would be conscious of the Holy Spirit's guidance and strength.

FURTHER STUDY

We sometimes make a distinction between Christians who obey the Word and those who are 'led by the Spirit' – what does the Bible say about that? Look at 2 Timothy 3:16–17; 1 Peter 1:10–12; 2 Peter 1:21.

People of the Trinity: unity in diversity

▶ INTRODUCTION

Does your church reflect the Trinity? The Godhead is one in essence and purpose, but each member has a different function. So reflecting the Trinity doesn't mean uniformity, and it doesn't mean merely avoiding church splits; it means experiencing unity and diversity within our community. This is one of the greatest struggles the church faces. We've got used to imitating the individualism of our age, pursuing independence instead of sharing our lives. Churches have become groups of individuals pursuing their own agendas, people whose priority is their family rather than the family of God; or clubs where you've got to have the same background and culture to be welcomed. So how can we get back to God's vision for the church?

READ *Ephesians 4:1-16*

[1]As a prisoner for the Lord, then, I urge you to live a life worthy of the calling you have received. [2]Be completely humble and gentle; be patient, bearing with one another in love. [3]Make every effort to keep the unity of the Spirit through the bond of peace. [4]There is one body and one Spirit, just as you were called to one hope when you were called; [5]one Lord, one faith, one baptism; [6]one God and Father of all, who is over all and through all and in all.

[7]But to each one of us grace has been given as Christ apportioned it. [8]This is why it says:

'When he ascended on high,
    he took many captives
    and gave gifts to his people.'

[9](What does 'he ascended' mean except that he also descended to the lower, earthly regions? [10]He who descended is the very one who ascended higher than all the heavens, in order to fill the whole universe.) [11]So Christ himself gave the apostles, the prophets, the evangelists, the pastors and teachers, [12]to equip his people for works of service, so that the body of Christ may be built up [13]until we all reach unity in the faith and in the knowledge of the Son of God and become mature, attaining to the whole measure of the fulness of Christ.

[14]Then we will no longer be infants, tossed back and forth by the waves, and blown here and there by every wind of teaching and by the cunning and craftiness of people in their deceitful scheming. [15]Instead, speaking the truth in love, we will grow to become in every respect the mature body of him who is the head, that is, Christ. [16]From him the whole body, joined and held together by every supporting ligament, grows and builds itself up in love, as each part does its work.

◉ FOCUS ON THE THEME

1.   In your experience, what destroys unity in the church?

◉ WHAT DOES THE BIBLE SAY?

2.   According to Ephesians 4:1–16, how can the church express its unity?

3.   What diversity does the passage tell us Paul expects in the church? What are the boundaries?

If one part [of the church] suffers, every part suffers with it; if one part is honoured, every part rejoices with it. Now you are the body of Christ, and each one of you is a part of it.   (1 Corinthians 12:26–27)

◉ INVESTIGATE FURTHER

4.   Read John 17:20–23. How are believers incorporated into the life of the Trinity?

5.   What impact will church unity have on the world?

 LIVING IT OUT

6.   Consider how you would promote unity and prize diversity in the following church scenarios:

- The older people want a traditional style of worship but the younger ones a more contemporary style.

- Some members are disagreeing about modes of baptism and the way the gifts of the Holy Spirit are expressed.

- Those from different parts of the world have different expectations of what church commitment looks like.

- Your friend doesn't go to homegroup. He says he hasn't got time and doesn't really like the intimacy of small groups.

7.   What would you say to a young person who has stopped coming to church because she wants to 'find herself'?

8.   When outsiders look at your church, what do they learn about the Trinity? What characteristics of the Father, Son and Holy Spirit are they seeing at work?

9.   Consider your own contribution to church life. How could you promote greater unity in your church?

The church is to be marked by the unity of God the Trinity. Our life together is to reflect that same love, mutual delight and other-person-centredness that characterizes the relationships of the Father, Son and Spirit. And as the world looks on, it will see what appear to be all sorts of irregularities, deviations from the normal paths of behaviour: Christians showing unworldly care and concern for one another. Hearts, wallets and homes cheerfully opened to help those in need. Those from backgrounds you wouldn't normally see together enjoying unity in Christ. Believers very different from one another but lit by a love of meeting, of praising their Saviour and taking his word to heart.

All these things should be deeply curious irregularities to a watching world . . . An undeniable sign that this community of believers is being held together by nothing less than a love that is divine in origin. The spectator who begins to extrapolate from these earth-bound irregularities will, in the end, be directed to the perfect heavenly analogue of them all.

The only explanation for a church like this can, ultimately, only be the reality of God the Trinity.   (Allberry, *Connected*, pp. 134–5)

 **PRAYER TIME**

Reflect on Jesus' prayer for unity in John 17. Pray for the various groups and ministries in your church. Pray that, although the church is made up of people with different personalities and gifts who serve God in different ways, your unity in Christ would be a powerful witness to outsiders.

 **FURTHER STUDY**

How does the Bible say that unity and diversity works out in marriage? Look at Genesis 1:26–27; Ephesians 5:22–32.

SESSION 6

Participating in the mission of the Trinity

▶ INTRODUCTION

From the earliest chapters of Genesis we see the unfolding of God's plan to bless the nations. The climax of this redemption plan was when the Father sent the Son, and together they sent the Spirit into our world. Now it's our turn. We join in the mission of the Trinity as God's ambassadors – speaking and living out the glorious good news of the gospel. The challenge is to discover your part in the plan. You have a mission field. Have you discovered where it is yet?

READ *Matthew 28:16-20*

¹⁶ Then the eleven disciples went to Galilee, to the mountain where Jesus had told them to go. ¹⁷ When they saw him, they worshipped him; but some doubted. ¹⁸ Then Jesus came to them and said, 'All authority in heaven and on earth has been given to me. ¹⁹ Therefore go and make disciples of all nations, baptising them in the name of the Father and of the Son and of the Holy Spirit, ²⁰ and teaching them to obey everything I have commanded you. And surely I am with you always, to the very end of the age.'

 ## FOCUS ON THE THEME

1. Write a job description for God – not what you would like him to do, but what he actually does. Then write a job description for yourself – again not what you would like to do, but what you actually do! Do you share the same goals and priorities?

 ## WHAT DOES THE BIBLE SAY?

2. How does Matthew 28:16–20 affirm the unity as well as the distinct roles of the Trinity?

3. What confidence does this passage give us for going out on mission?

4.   What is the goal of mission?

The baptismal formula of Jesus, which would be repeated down through the ages in countless baptisms, and the apostolic benediction in Paul (2 Corinthians 13:14), which would be repeated in countless acts of worship, make it clear that this is a truth God wants to preserve at the forefront of the church's consciousness at all times and in all places.

(Lewis, *Message of the Living God*, p. 283)

⊙ INVESTIGATE FURTHER

5.   In John 20:21 Jesus says, 'As the Father has sent me, I am sending you.'

- In what way is our mission the same as Jesus'?

- How are the disciples equipped for the task (v. 22)?

The reality of God as the Father, the Son and the Holy Spirit is the first truth of all mission and the gospel cannot be preached adequately without it. The message of the good news is that 'God so loved the world that he gave his one and only Son, that whoever believes in him shall not perish but have eternal life,' and it is in the power of the Holy Spirit that the light of that truth enters the minds and the joy of that truth grasps the heart. Trinitarian truth lies at the core of the gospel and is implicit in its first proclamation. (Lewis, *Message of the Living God*, pp. 291–2)

6.   How does Paul describe our role in mission in 2 Corinthians 5:18–20?

♥ LIVING IT OUT

7.   The Bible teaches there is only one God. How should this truth affect how we share the gospel with:

  •   People from different religions?

  •   People from different social/cultural backgrounds?

8.   What good news about the Trinity can we share with the following individuals?

  •   A person searching to find identity and meaning in life

  •   A Muslim who cannot have a relationship with his god Allah who is remote

9.   How does sharing the gospel help explain the mystery of the Trinity to non-Christians?

10.   Are you participating in the mission of the Trinity? Where is your mission field?

▲ PRAYER TIME

Bring your mission field to God. Pray for the friends, family and people in your sphere of influence who need to hear the gospel. Ask God to bring five people to mind – pray daily for these 'top five' to accept the gospel. Pray for each person in the group that they would obey the Holy Spirit's prompting, be bold in sharing the gospel, use wise words in conversation, and live holy lives that authenticate the message.

● FURTHER STUDY

Trace God's missionary purpose and desire to bless the nations throughout Scripture. Look at Genesis 12:1–5; Psalm 96; Isaiah 2:1–3; John 1:1–14; Revelation 5:9.

SESSION 7

Living in the power of the Trinity

▶ INTRODUCTION

We often get wistful when we read the Acts of the Apostles, longing to get back to the glory days of the early church. So Paul would probably want to remind us that the same Holy Spirit power that raised Jesus from the dead is living in us (Ephesians 1:18–20). The Holy Spirit who performed miracles, who enabled frightened fishermen to boldly proclaim the gospel, who urged people to share their possessions and give to the poor, who built the church, who transformed lives – he is the power of the Trinity living in us, available to us. The Holy Spirit might not work in the same way at all times, but his power is just as real within us as it was within the early Christians.

READ *Acts 2:1-8, 12-24, 32-33, 36-39*

(1–8) ¹*When the day of Pentecost came, they were all together in one place. ²Suddenly a sound like the blowing of a violent wind came from heaven and filled the whole house where they were sitting. ³They saw what seemed to be tongues of fire that separated and came to rest on each of them. ⁴All of them were filled with the Holy Spirit and began to speak in other tongues as the Spirit enabled them.*

⁵*Now there were staying in Jerusalem God-fearing Jews from every nation under heaven. ⁶When they heard this sound, a crowd came together in bewilderment, because each one heard their own language being spoken. ⁷Utterly amazed, they asked: 'Aren't all these who are speaking Galileans? ⁸Then how is it that each of us hears them in our native language?'*

(12–24) ¹²*Amazed and perplexed, they asked one another, 'What does this mean?'*

¹³*Some, however, made fun of them and said, 'They have had too much wine.'*

¹⁴*Then Peter stood up with the Eleven, raised his voice and addressed the crowd: 'Fellow Jews and all of you who live in Jerusalem, let me explain this to you; listen carefully to what I say. ¹⁵These people are not drunk, as you suppose. It's only nine in the morning! ¹⁶No, this is what was spoken by the prophet Joel:*

> ¹⁷*"In the last days, God says,*
>   *I will pour out my Spirit on all people.*
> *Your sons and daughters will prophesy,*
>   *your young men will see visions,*
>   *your old men will dream dreams.*
> ¹⁸*Even on my servants, both men and women,*
>   *I will pour out my Spirit in those days,*
>   *and they will prophesy.*
> ¹⁹*I will show wonders in the heavens above*
>   *and signs on the earth below,*
>   *blood and fire and billows of smoke.*

²⁰*The sun will be turned to darkness*
and the moon to blood
before the coming of the great and glorious day of the Lord.
²¹*And everyone who calls*
on the name of the Lord will be saved.'

²²*'Fellow Israelites, listen to this: Jesus of Nazareth was a man accredited by God to you by miracles, wonders and signs, which God did among you through him, as you yourselves know.* ²³*This man was handed over to you by God's deliberate plan and foreknowledge; and you, with the help of wicked men, put him to death by nailing him to the cross.* ²⁴*But God raised him from the dead, freeing him from the agony of death, because it was impossible for death to keep its hold on him . . . '*

(32–33) ³²*'God has raised this Jesus to life, and we are all witnesses of it.* ³³*Exalted to the right hand of God, he has received from the Father the promised Holy Spirit and has poured out what you now see and hear . . . '*

(36–39) ³⁶*'Therefore let all Israel be assured of this: God has made this Jesus, whom you crucified, both Lord and Messiah.'*

³⁷*When the people heard this, they were cut to the heart and said to Peter and the other apostles, 'Brothers, what shall we do?'*

³⁸*Peter replied, 'Repent and be baptised, every one of you, in the name of Jesus Christ for the forgiveness of your sins. And you will receive the gift of the Holy Spirit.* ³⁹*The promise is for you and your children and for all who are far off – for all whom the Lord our God will call.'*

⊙ FOCUS ON THE THEME

1. What are the telltale signs that we are living or serving God in our own strength rather than relying on the Holy Spirit?

🔍 WHAT DOES THE BIBLE SAY?

2. What effect did the Holy Spirit have on the disciples? Look at verses 4, 8, 14, 17–18.

3. What did the prophet Joel say about the Holy Spirit?

4. What promise did Peter give future believers in verses 38–39?

◎ INVESTIGATE FURTHER

5. Look at Ephesians 3:14–19.

   • Why does Paul ask for Holy Spirit power?

   • How is this different from what we ask for power for?

6. According to Paul's prayer, how are the Father, Son and Holy Spirit working in our hearts?

7.   In what ways does the Holy Spirit empower us for service today?
     Look at:

     - Romans 8:13

     - Romans 8:26

     - 1 Corinthians 12:7, 11

♥ LIVING IT OUT

8.   What spiritual gifts or resources do you think God has given you?
     It may help to look at the gifts lists in Romans 12:6–8; 1 Corinthians
     12:27–31; 1 Peter 4:10–11 (although these lists are not exhaustive).
     Also ask other group members what spiritual gifts they think you
     have.

9.   Consider your own situation. In what particular ways do you need
     the Holy Spirit's help and power?

10. How can we relate to Ephesians 3:20–21 when life is hard, we are
     struggling, and God doesn't seem to be doing 'immeasurably more
     than all we ask or imagine'?

▲ PRAYER TIME

Pray Ephesians 3:14–21 for one another. In particular, pray that you would know the Holy Spirit's strength, you would rely on God's resources, and that, whatever the situation, you would trust that God is working all things out for his glory.

> *God can do anything, you know – far more than you could ever imagine or guess or request in your wildest dreams! He does it not by pushing us around but by working within us, his Spirit deeply and gently within us.*
>
> > *Glory to God in the church!*
> > *Glory to God in the Messiah, in Jesus!*
> > *Glory down all the generations!*
> > *Glory through all millennia! Oh, yes!*
>
> (Ephesians 3:20–21 MSG)

● FURTHER STUDY

Look at the key passages which talk about spiritual gifts: Romans 12:4–8; 1 Corinthians 12; 1 Peter 4:10–11. What themes do the Bible writers emphasize?

Leader's guide

As a leader, your role is not to answer every question but to facilitate group discussion and to help people focus on what God's Word says. Make sure you make time during the week to read the Bible passages and questions. Look at the leader's guide and see how best to present the questions and generate discussion.

If you are to make the most of your group time, it is a great help if each group member can read the passage and think about the subject of the study in advance. Of course, this is difficult when members don't have much time to sit down and prepare. To help with this, there is a short supplement for each study. You can sign up your group members to receive this in advance of each week's study. It includes the passage to be studied, as well as something to help the reader begin to think about the subject of the week's study. They are very short, simple, and accessible, ideal for busy people. See **www.ivpbooks.com/transformingtrinity** for a sample.

The supplement is automatically delivered each week to those who have signed up, either as an ebook, email or a pdf which is easily readable or printable. See the website for further details of how to receive it.

Don't rush through the study; feel free to miss some questions out and focus on what's most pertinent to your group. The aim is not just to learn about the Trinity but to see how it impacts our lives and is crucial to our faith.

Be aware of the group dynamics. Some people are eager to contribute and others less so. You may have to encourage quieter folk to participate and ask the more vocal ones to listen! Invite a number of replies to each question so that people share what they have prepared and learn from one another's responses.

It is important to leave time at the end of the session for prayer and to sum up what God has taught you. Make sure the group members go home clear about the main message of the study and how they are going to apply it in their lives in the coming week.

Your group may be well established and your members prepared to talk at a deep level. New groups take time to settle but, as your group members get to know one another, you'll not just be talking about the Trinity but experiencing the true community of the Trinity as you discuss, share and pray together.

They are not integral to the study, but the 2013 Keswick Convention talks on 'The Transforming Trinity' are available on DVD or CD and can be downloaded free at www.keswickministries.org. Leaders, individuals or your small group could use these to complement the study. If you would like to do some wider reading there are a number of books available: Tim Chester's *Delighting in the Trinity* and Sam Allberry's *Connected* are both helpful and accessible.

Saved by the triune God

1. Encourage group members to talk about their struggles and questions about the Trinity. Come back to these issues as they are addressed in subsequent studies.

2. Help the group to see the different functions but interdependence of the members of the Trinity. Father – in love he chose us to be his children; in his grace and wisdom he sent Jesus to die on our behalf. Son – Jesus' death on the cross has redeemed us; he forgives our sin. Holy Spirit – a seal or guarantee of our full redemption and home in heaven.

3. Contrary to popular opinion, the Father is not some distant, aloof figure. God the Father is lovingly involved in our salvation which he has planned from eternity. He has generously and kindly blessed us – because of our union with Christ we already have all the spiritual blessings we need. Out of love the Father sent Jesus, whom he loved, to save us. He chose us; he adopted us as his children, to enjoy an intimate, personal relationship with him. God's wisdom and pleasure is seen in the revelation and accomplishment of his salvation plan.

4. All three members of the Trinity work together for our salvation – so that we would be God's sons and daughters (v. 5), we would be redeemed (v. 7), we would acknowledge Christ's headship (v. 10) and we would bring God glory (vv. 12, 14). The Trinity is united in purpose and will.

5. God the Father is the one who sends Jesus and orchestrates the salvation plan. Jesus willingly came to earth to preach repentance and to tell people how they could get right with God. The Holy Spirit enters people's lives when they repent. The Holy Spirit was also on Jesus, empowering him for ministry, sending him out into the desert. Notice God the Father's love of the Son and his appreciation of him

before he had done any ministry. Right at the start of the gospel, we see all three members of the Trinity in loving community, working together, fulfilling their different roles, to make salvation possible for us.

6a. Because Jesus was fully God he was holy and sinless. This means he was an effective substitute – on the cross he did not die for his own sin, but he was able to die for ours. Unlike other priests, Jesus' sacrifice was a once-and-for-all act: it is eternally effective.

b. Jesus was also fully human. This means he was able to die in our place; he was an acceptable substitute. By becoming one of us, Jesus was able to represent us before God.

If we don't affirm the full deity and humanity of Christ, we fall into the trap of seeing Jesus as less than God, even as an unwilling victim in God's plan of salvation.

7. Philippians 2:5–11 teaches us that Jesus was fully God. With regard to his divinity, he was the same 'nature' or essence as God. However, he did not hold on to the privilege, status and glory he enjoyed with the Father before his incarnation, but gave it up to win our salvation. Jesus was obedient to the Father, coming to earth and dying on a cross (v. 8). God exalts Jesus and wants everyone to worship and serve Jesus as Lord.

8. The triune God does not stop working after we are saved – all three members of the Trinity assure us of our salvation and help us grow as disciples. God helps us stand firm and stay faithful. We are 'in Christ'; we have an unbreakable union with him. And the Holy Spirit in us is a guarantee that one day our salvation will be complete.

9. God the Father knows all about suffering because he gave his Son, whom he loved, to die for us. Jesus was not just God's representative; he was God himself entering the pain of our world, dying in our place on the cross. The cross shows us how much God loved us. And the Trinity itself – a loving community of the Godhead – shows that God is a loving, personal God. A proper view of the Trinity is therefore

essential for our evangelism and to address comments such as 'If there was a God, he would do something about the suffering in the world.'

10. God does not ignore our sin or brush it aside. At the cross he dealt with it decisively. The only way for God's wrath to be appeased and for sin to be forgiven was for God himself, in the person of Jesus, to die in our place. Being fully God and fully human, Jesus was a perfect sacrifice for our sin. So even if Satan reminds us of our sin, or if we live with the consequences of it, we can know that we are forgiven and redeemed. Understanding the Trinity is crucial if we are going to experience the assurance of sins forgiven and freedom from guilt.

Knowing the Father

1. Each member of the group will have a different response to the term 'Father', depending on his or her own experience. Some fathers were absent, some loving, some authoritarian, some distant, some indulging, some Christians, some unbelievers. However good our experience of an earthly father is, God gives us a full and true picture of fatherhood.

2. We become children of God by believing in Christ's work for us on the cross. Paul explains this as having faith in Christ, being baptized into Christ, being clothed with Christ and belonging to Christ. These descriptions highlight the union we have with Christ once we become Christians. When we have faith in Christ, we share in his death, resurrection and righteousness. Because we are 'in Christ', like Jesus, we are sons and daughters of God.

3. The Holy Spirit working in our lives is the guarantee that we are children of God. The Spirit helps us recognize our sonship and enjoy intimacy with God as our Father. *Abba* is a familiar term, like 'Daddy'.

4. The passage in Galatians compares the status of a slave to a child in the household. The point is that as believers we are children of God, adopted into his family, sharing a relationship with the Father that a slave never could. However, all people, whether Christians or not, are slaves. We all serve what we prize most and invest our lives in. Christians are no longer slaves to sin – the penalty for sin and its power over us has been broken by Jesus' death on the cross. We are now free to become slaves of righteousness – in the Holy Spirit's power, obeying God and pursuing holy lives.

5. Matthew 7:7–11 shows us that God is approachable. He is interested in us and he wants to hear our prayers. He wants us to keep coming to him continually – not only turning to him when we have huge issues to deal with. God is better than the best of fathers – he wants to give

good gifts to his children. This doesn't mean we always get what we want; rather God gives us what he knows is best for us. Ephesians 3:14 reminds us that, as well as being familiar with God, we should also approach him reverently, in submission, remembering who he is.

6. Our status as children of God is not up for negotiation, but John urges us to continue growing as Christians, becoming more Christlike, so we will be ready for Jesus' return. Jesus' return must be like a beacon: always guiding our behaviour, ordering our priorities and giving us hope. Our lives must be marked by holy living, right actions, a desire to wrestle with sin and a love for fellow believers.

7. In hard times it helps to remember we are secure and safe as God's children, held in the palm of his hand. God has already shown how much he loves us by sending Jesus to die in our place. We are now part of God's family and, as Galatians reminds us, we have a sure inheritance that is worth waiting for. As we look forward to that day, we know that God is with us in our struggles; he may not change our situation, but he will use it to refine us and for his glory.

8. The fact that God is our Father reminds us we can approach him at any time about anything. He is concerned about us; he listens to us; we can come to him boldly. He wants to give us good gifts. Like earthly fathers, he will not give us everything we want, but he will give us what is good for us. With God as our Father we can enjoy intimacy with the God of heaven and earth – what an amazing privilege!

9. If it is appropriate, invite the members of your group to share their answers. Discuss how what you have learnt from the study will change how you relate to God in the future.

Following the Son

1. Obviously it's our heart relationship with Jesus that makes us a Christian, but that relationship should impact the rest of our lives. If someone came to stay at our home, they should be able to tell we are a Christian by our conversations, the programmes we watch or don't watch on TV, the books we read and the way we interact with our children/parents. How we spend our time and money, as well as our values and aspirations, should all point people to our faith in God.

2. The man was trying to get to heaven by living a morally upright life, obeying all the requirements of the law, externally conforming to expectations. The man was trying to earn or work his way into heaven. He didn't realize that no-one would ever be good enough by their own righteousness to get into heaven. He failed to understand that eternal life is a gift given by God and that all he could do was trust God fully for it.

3. The Bible teaches that we are to look after the poor (for example Romans 15:26; Galatians 2:10). However, selling everything we have is not a prerequisite for salvation. Jesus wanted this man to get rid of his wealth because he loved it more than God. Becoming a follower of Christ is not a matter of following rules. Rather it is to surrender our wills to him, relinquishing all we prize above him.

4. It is hard for rich people to be saved because they have more to surrender to Christ. However, all things are possible with God! God can save rich and poor, because the blood of Christ avails for all. No-one can earn their way into heaven – salvation is a gift from God.

5. God is no-one's debtor. He will more than recompense us for whatever we give up for Christ's sake, in this life as well as in the future. For example, if we have left family to become a Christian or to share the gospel, we will receive fellowship and support from the church family. As well as these blessings there will be persecution, but we look forward to the triumph of eternal life.

6. When God talks about the oneness or unity in the Godhead, he combines it with talking about the need for our wholehearted, integrated devotion. 'The observation that God is one is not incidental to what follows. It is the ground for it. The Lord our God is one. *Therefore* we are to love him with all that we are and all that we have. His oneness and the totality of our love for him are tightly bound together' (Allberry, *Connected*, p. 24).

7. We are to imitate Jesus' obedience to God in all situations. Like Jesus, we must make sure that doing God's will and his work is the central pursuit of our lives.

8. There are many areas of life that we have trouble surrendering to God – our children, our finances, problems in family relationships. Perhaps we are worried what God will ask us to do if we surrender our children to him. Perhaps we want to deal with situations on our own. We want to be in control and we don't want to wait for God to act. Sometimes we don't even realize we are not surrendering specific areas of our life to God. We may have talked with our husband/wife about a problem with the children and come up with a plan of action, but we haven't actually prayed about it. We haven't actually committed the situation to God.

9. This discussion is not intended to be a guilt trip! We all have areas in our lives which, intentionally or unintentionally, we don't surrender to God. We get used to compartmentalizing our lives. Use this time to examine your life and reflect on areas you need to change.

10. As a group, come up with some practical examples of how you can be more wholehearted in your devotion to Christ. For example, regularly assessing your spiritual progress; repenting and asking for the Holy Spirit's help to make changes; getting into a prayer triplet or accountability group to spur one another on in the faith; daily reading God's Word to purify your heart.

Walking in the Spirit

1. The Bible describes 'the Holy Spirit' as wind, a dove, and tongues of fire. These images help us understand more about his character. The wind portrays the Holy Spirit as powerful, mysterious and uncontainable. Tongues of fire represent the divinity and holiness of the Spirit. The dove reminds us that the Holy Spirit is full of gentleness, purity and peace.

2. The passage is describing Christians and non-Christians. Non-Christians are those who live according to their sinful nature, hostile towards God and unable to please him. Christians are described as belonging to Christ, having Christ in us, being sons of God and God's children. When we are saved, the Holy Spirit dwells in us and helps us live to please God. It is not that believers are better people than unbelievers – salvation is an act of God's amazing grace.

3. The Holy Spirit, the same power who raised Jesus from the dead, is given to believers. The Holy Spirit is the guarantee that our bodies will be raised like Christ's (vv. 10–11). The Spirit helps us say 'no' to sin and 'yes' to holy living (v. 13). The Spirit also encourages us that we belong to God, we are his children and we can approach him without fear (vv. 15–16).

4. The Holy Spirit empowers us to say 'no' to sin and 'yes' to righteousness. However, we have to 'put to death' these sins – it is our responsibility to deal ruthlessly with sin. We must work in conjunction with the Holy Spirit – we cannot be holy in our own strength, and the Spirit will not make us holy without our effort. See also Philippians 2:13; Romans 12:1.

5. If we are living by the Spirit, we have a desire to be holy and avoid sin. We will be producing the fruit of the Spirit – our attitudes and behaviour will change as we increasingly develop a Christlike

character marked by godliness. We recognize that our identification with Christ means we have put to death our old self – our selfish desires and passions – and, in the Holy Spirit's power, live worthy of God. We have been made spiritually alive by the Holy Spirit, so now we need to keep living in line with his values and priorities. Paul gives us a very practical example of what this looks like in verse 26.

6. In a sense, believers are free to live as they please because, as they submit to God and are led by the Holy Spirit, they will want to be holy in their actions and attitudes. As St Augustine said, 'Love God; then do whatever you want.' Romans 8:4 – obeying the law cannot save us or make us holy, but we obey God in the Holy Spirit's power because we want to please him. We cannot keep the whole law, but all the requirements of the law were met in Christ.

7. There are no short cuts to keeping in step with the Spirit and growing in holiness. Rather it is a matter of making every effort to get rid of sin and to deal ruthlessly with it in the Spirit's power (Hebrews 12:1). We also need to cultivate holy habits: Psalm 1 talks of Bible reading and meditating on God's Word; Philippians 4 encourages us to pray; Hebrews 10:24–25 exhorts us to keep meeting with other Christians for fellowship. We need to pursue these disciplines daily so that they shape our actions and attitudes. The image of keeping in step or walking with the Spirit implies a continuous, unspectacular pursuit rather like practising the spiritual disciplines.

8. Realizing the Holy Spirit is a distinct person takes us away from the notion that he is a magical force, invoked in emergencies, and only by those with a special connection to the spiritual realm. In fact every believer can develop a personal relationship with the Holy Spirit – learning to hear his voice, recognize his promptings and rely on his power. As in any personal relationship, we can grieve the Holy Spirit or we can strengthen our bond with him.

9. • We could remind the believer trapped in a cycle of sin that he can be free through the power of the Holy Spirit (Galatians 5:16). Freedom from sin is not merely a matter of trying harder; it is also

relying on God's power. Perhaps point him to Romans 6:11–14 which explains that fighting sin is a two-pronged attack: removing the sin and temptation but also filling our lives with godliness through Bible reading, prayer, fellowship, accountability, etc. Also reflect on Philippians 4:8.

- Pastoral sensitivity is required in all these discussions, but particularly when talking to the apathetic Christian. Perhaps this individual has never actually been saved, in which case there is no reason to see evidence of the Holy Spirit. Or perhaps this Christian has cut herself off from the power and presence of the Spirit – she has stopped reading her Bible, praying, attending church; she has grieved the Spirit in some way and so gradually her heart has grown cold. Discuss what happened and why she feels far away from God – perhaps a challenge is in order?

- A Christian who is seeking God, desiring to be holy and obeying the Scriptures, cannot help but walk 'in step with the Spirit.' Encourage this believer to keep pursuing God, talk to mature Christians about these important decisions, take logical steps and trust that, as he is obedient to all that God has revealed to him, he will be 'in step with the Spirit.'

10. Essentially this is personalizing the answers to question 8. Encourage the group to come up with personal, concrete responses that you can then use in the prayer time together.

SESSION 5

People of the Trinity: unity in diversity

1. Unity can be destroyed by all sorts of things. For example, gossip; jealousy of someone else's material possessions or spiritual gifts; bitterness because of past hurts; criticism of church leaders. Unity can also be destroyed as we unconsciously import values from our culture such as pursuing individuality or uniformity. Uniformity is evident when everyone in the church comes from the same background; no other cultures or backgrounds are welcomed. We also see uniformity when leaders wrestle to keep everything in their control, not letting others express their gifts.

2. Each of us can express our commitment to unity by being patient and humble, and bearing with one another in love. Treating one another kindly and compassionately goes a long way to preserve unity in the church. Also not being jealous of others' spiritual gifts but acknowledging they are for the benefit of the body of Christ. Unity is expressed by our adherence to the core truths about God; our commitment to press on to maturity and develop a Christlike character; our acknowledgment that Christ, not us, is the head of the church.

3. In Ephesians Paul is talking about spiritual gifts. He gives a sample list here to show the variety of gifts God gives to the church. But there are boundaries or right ways to use these gifts. Using your spiritual gift is not an excuse for showing off or making others feel inferior. There is no point in envying other people's gifts or thinking your gift is so small it's not worth getting involved in church life. We all have different gifts and different roles to play. As we exercise our gifts, we must remember that we are just parts of the body, while Christ is the head: 'From him the whole body . . . grows and builds itself up in love' (v. 16).

4. The Father, Son and Holy Spirit share one divine nature and so the Father is 'in' the Son, and the Son is 'in' the Father. When we become Christians we are incorporated into the life of this divine community; we participate in the Trinity. That means God the Father loves us with the same love as he loves Jesus. It means that, through the Holy Spirit, Jesus is 'in' us. 'We are part of the family. The Father is our Father. The Son is our Brother. The Spirit indwells us' (Chester, *Delighting in the Trinity*, p. 167).

5. Church unity modelled on the unity in the Godhead will show the world that God sent Jesus as part of his salvation plan and that God loves the world as he loves his own Son. Our unity will have an evangelistic impact.

6. Encourage the group to come up with some practical responses to these church issues. Discuss how we can be humble, patient and Christlike while disagreeing with other church members. What core issues must we unite around? How can we maintain a godly attitude when we disagree? How can we ensure we are not confusing uniformity with unity?

7. Many people say they are Christians but don't need or want to come to church. Often people say they want to engage in some solitary soul-searching in order to 'find themselves'. The Trinity blows these two notions apart. We are made in the image of God and God is a community. If we are going to find our true identity and understand what it means to be human, it is going to be in relation to other people. Community is especially important for Christians – we need to live out the truth of John 17:20–23; we need to display the unity and diversity of the Godhead to a watching world. We can't grow as believers without spurring one another on, denying ourselves for the sake of others, and bearing one another's burdens.

8. Are outsiders able to see God's love in action when they come into the church – are they welcomed genuinely and looked after? Do they see the selflessness of Jesus in the way we care for those on the margins of society? Do they see the Holy Spirit at work in our hearts, uniting a

disparate group of people together for worship and ministry? Discuss honestly what image your church portrays to outsiders. Do people look at your church and think there is no explanation for your behaviour other than God's love?

9. Follow on from question 8 and explore how we can reflect the Trinity more fully and genuinely work towards unity in our church fellowships. While being sensitive to any current issues in the church, try to be as honest as possible in your discussions.

SESSION 6

Participating in the mission of the Trinity

1. God's priority is his own glory (Romans 11:36). Saving, healing, making us holy and everything else God does is for his glory. As his children we need to share this priority. We should see our life not as a string of unrelated activities but as a whole where God's glory is reflected in every aspect – how we bring up our children, how we uphold God's values at work, how we share in community life, how we share the gospel, etc.

2. The unity of the Trinity is seen in verse 19 – we are to be baptized 'in *the* name of the Father and of the Son and of the Holy Spirit' (emphasis added). The 'name' is singular. We also see the distinct roles of the Trinity – the Father gave all authority to Jesus; baptism was a sign of identification with Jesus in his death and resurrection; and through the Holy Spirit's power Jesus would be always with the disciples.

3. We, like the apostles, share the gospel on Jesus' authority. Jesus commands us to tell others about him. When we do so, we can be confident that God is with us and equipping us for service through the power of the Holy Spirit.

4. The goal of mission is not just to share the good news but to make disciples: mature, devoted followers of Christ. As believers are baptized, they affirm they have died to sin and want to live a new, Christ-centred life. We are to teach these new converts – not just with words but with our lives – what it means to follow Christ.

5. • Jesus was sent by the Father to preach the good news and make it available to us. He died and rose again to pay the punishment for our sins. We are to go into the world like Jesus did – responding to God's call, obeying in the strength of the Holy Spirit, with the aim of drawing others to Christ through our words and lives. This verse indicates we are to carry on Jesus' gospel mission now he has returned to heaven.

- The disciples needed the Holy Spirit to fulfil God's mission – and so do we.

6. Paul explains that we have been given the ministry of reconciliation – we must tell people how they can know peace with God. We have been reconciled to God so now we have to pass this message on; we cannot keep it to ourselves. Paul says we are God's ambassadors – we represent him to non-Christians and they learn what God is like by watching us. Paul highlights the urgency and responsibility of our task.

7. • We must always be very prayerful and sensitive when we share the gospel. Many people believe in other gods, but according to the Bible these gods are not real. Therefore there is an urgency to share the gospel; people are looking for salvation in all the wrong places and we need to present them with the truth.

   • There is one God and only one way to be saved by God – by believing in the death and resurrection of Jesus and surrendering our life to him. This is the criterion and we must not put any other barriers in the way of people coming to Jesus. They do not have to dress like us, have the same education as us, or be the same ethnicity as us!

8. • People may not state explicitly that they are searching for meaning and identity, but many are. The gospel isn't about 'finding ourselves', but a result of our sins being forgiven is that in our new relationship with Christ we join the Trinity as well as the church. We find meaning and identity through these communities. Our life is no longer measured by what we achieve but by our obedience to Christ – this is liberating!

   • Allah is a remote god who must be obeyed. He cannot identify with his followers. In the Trinity we have a God who shares our sorrows and comforts us, and yet is sovereign. Having a triune God means we have a God who is 'with us' but who also rules the universe. Theologians call these attributes of God his *immanence* and *transcendence*.

9. We don't need to labour the concept of the Trinity. It arises naturally as we share the gospel with unbelievers. We explain that God sent his Son Jesus into the world to save us from our sins, and we accept and live in the truth of this message through the power of the Holy Spirit. In the church, people can also see the Trinity in action – they will see us obeying God's will, loving him as Father, trusting in Christ's death for salvation, empowered by the Holy Spirit for service.

10. Where is your mission field? For some of us it could be abroad, but for others it will be at home with family, neighbours and work colleagues. Consider the context where God has placed you, the people he has put into your life and the work he has given you. Try to see your employment situation, family life and friendship groups with fresh eyes – God's eyes.

SESSION 7

Living in the power of the Trinity

1. When we try to serve God in our own strength, we find ourselves running on empty. We can become critical of others, lose patience, get anxious about results, feel the pressure to perform and be overwhelmed with all that needs to be done. The focus is on us and what we are achieving rather than on God, trusting that he has equipped us for our unique service.

2. When the Holy Spirit came, the apostles were able to speak in different languages so that all the people in Jerusalem for the Passover could hear the gospel in their own tongue. Peter was given boldness to preach and clearly explain the good news. Believers were also given the gift of prophecy, and saw dreams and visions. (It's easy to get into a debate whether the gift of tongues exists today and whether it is a foreign language or a private prayer language. This may be an interesting discussion, but be careful not to let it unsettle the group or cause divisions – especially if your church has a position on this. Rather, encourage the group to see the 'equipping nature' of the Holy Spirit's power.)

3. Joel emphasized that the Holy Spirit would come on all believers regardless of gender, age or rank. People would prophesy, see visions and dream dreams. While the Holy Spirit would come on individuals, it would affect the whole church community – equipping believers, building unity and pointing others to Christ (v. 21).

4. The same Holy Spirit who empowered the apostles for service and gave Peter boldness to preach is given to us. When we become Christians we receive the Holy Spirit (see Ephesians 1:13–14) and he enables us to serve God, just as he empowered Jesus and the apostles.

5. • Paul prays that the Holy Spirit would give us power to understand how much Jesus loves us. He also prays that the Holy Spirit would help us open our lives more fully to Jesus. The end result is that we will be filled with the fullness of God.

- Perhaps we pray more readily for power to accomplish tasks for God, but it's worth remembering that God is more interested in the state of our hearts and our devotion to him. The Holy Spirit wants to transform us, strengthen us and make us more like Christ – not just to help us accomplish tasks.

6. It is out of the Father's great riches that he strengthens us to live godly lives. He sends the Holy Spirit to strengthen our hearts and Christ to indwell them. The aim is for the church body to know Christ's love and be filled with all the fullness of God. This passage shows us the three persons of the Trinity at work, equipping us for holiness, filling us with God's love, enabling us to rely on his resources so we can fulfil his mission in the world.

7. • Romans 8:13 – the Holy Spirit helps us tackle sin in our lives.

   • Romans 8:26 – the Holy Spirit helps us pray, especially when we don't know what to say because we are not sure what God's will is.

   • 1 Corinthians 12:7, 11 – he gives spiritual gifts for service to equip believers and build up the body of Christ. The Holy Spirit determines who receives each gift, so there is no room for jealousy or feelings of inferiority.

8. Encourage the group to recognize the 'behind the scenes' gifts as well as the upfront, prominent ones. Affirm each member of the group – everyone has at least one spiritual gift given for the building up of the body of Christ. If people are unsure of their spiritual gifts, encourage them to do a 'Discovering your gifts' course; try out different areas of service; speak to mature believers who have observed them serving; reflect on what areas they most enjoy serving in. God has also given us resources we can use to serve him – money, time, intellect, homes; consider all that God has given you and how he wants you to use it in his service.

9. Marry the truths of God's Word to your own situation. You are indwelt by the Holy Spirit; you have all the resources you need to live for God in the situation he has placed you – so where do you need his

help and power? Perhaps in sharing the gospel with a family member, upholding godly values at work, raising your children, looking after elderly relatives, trusting God for church finances or a new building project.

10. These two verses sum up the first half of the book of Ephesians. They help us remember that God's power is at work in us – we should not lose sight of this but must rely on it. The verses also remind us that God's ultimate goal is his glory – we don't always know how our prayer requests and life situations fit in with his great plan, but we trust that God is doing more than we could ever imagine, and his plan will culminate marvellously to bring glory to himself.

Bibliography

Allberry, Sam, *Connected: Living in the Light of the Trinity* (IVP, 2012).

Bavinck, Herman, *The Doctrine of God*, tr. William Hendriksen (Eerdmans, 1951), reprint edition (Banner of Truth, 1971).

Berkhof, Louis, *Systematic Theology*, 4th ed. (Eerdmans, 1939).

Chester, Tim, *Delighting in the Trinity: Why Father, Son and Spirit Are Good News*, 2nd ed. (The Good Book Company, 2010).

Lewis, Peter, *The Message of the Living God* (IVP, 2000).

About Keswick Ministries

Keswick Ministries is committed to the deepening of the spiritual life in individuals and church communities through the careful exposition and application of Scripture, seeking to encourage the following:

- **Lordship of Christ** – to encourage submission to the Lordship of Christ in personal and corporate living

- **Life Transformation** – to encourage a dependency upon the indwelling and fullness of the Holy Spirit for life transformation and effective living

- **Evangelism and Mission** – to provoke a strong commitment to the breadth of evangelism and mission in the British Isles and worldwide

- **Discipleship** – to stimulate the discipling and training of people of all ages in godliness, service and sacrificial living

- **Unity** – to provide a practical demonstration of evangelical unity

Keswick Ministries is committed to achieving its aims by:

- providing Bible-based training courses for youth workers and young people (via Root 66) and Bible Weeks for Christians of all backgrounds who want to develop their skills and learn more

- promoting the use of books, DVDs, CDs and downloads so that Keswick's teaching ministry is brought to a wider audience at home and abroad

- producing TV and radio programmes so that superb Bible talks can be broadcast to you at home

- publishing up-to-date details of Keswick's exciting news and events on our website so that you can access material and purchase Keswick products online

- publicizing Bible-teaching events in the UK and overseas so that Christians of all ages are encouraged to attend 'Keswick' meetings closer to home and grow in their faith

- putting the residential accommodation of the Convention Centre at the disposal of churches, youth groups, Christian organizations, and many others, at very reasonable rates, for holidays and outdoor activities in a stunning location

If you'd like more details, please look at our website
(www.keswickministries.org)
or contact the Keswick Ministries office
by post, email or telephone as given below.

**Keswick Ministries, Convention Centre, Skiddaw Street,
Keswick, Cumbria CA12 4BY
Tel: 01768 780075; Fax: 01768 775276;
email: info@keswickministries.org**

Keswick Convention 2014

Really?

Searching for reality in a confusing world

- Is God really necessary, if science is everything?
- Is God really there, as so many suffer?
- Is Jesus really unique, with so many faiths?

In a wireless world of endless explanations, is it really possible to discover ultimate reality? And is it really credible to believe that it's found in Jesus Christ?

The answers may not be the last word, but they will be honest and biblical and suitable for both convinced Christians and intrigued enquirers.

Week 1: 12 July – 18 July
Week 2: 19 July – 25 July
Week 3: 26 July – 1 August

Check out the website for further details:
www.keswickministries.org

also by Elizabeth McQuoid

The Amazing Cross
Transforming lives today
Jeremy & Elizabeth McQuoid

ISBN: 978-1-84474-587-6
192 pages, paperback

The cross of Christ is the heartbeat of Christianity. It is a place of pain and horror, wonder and beauty, all at the same time. It is the place where our sin collided gloriously with God's grace.

But do we really understand what the cross is all about? Or are we so caught up in the peripherals of the faith that we have forgotten the core? We need to ask ourselves:

- How deep an impact has the cross made on my personality?
- Do I live in the light of the freedom it has won for me?
- Am I dying to myself every day, so that I can live for Christ?
- Do I face suffering with faith and assurance?
- Can I face death in the light of the hope of the resurrection?

The authors present us with a contemporary challenge to place all of our lives, every thought, word and deed, under the shadow of the amazing cross, and allow that cross to transform us here and now.

'It is an ideal introduction to the heart of the Christian gospel, and a very welcome addition to the Keswick Foundation series.' Jonathan Lamb

Available from your local Christian bookshop or **www.thinkivp.com**

For more information about IVP
and our publications visit

www.ivpbooks.com

Get regular updates at **ivpbooks.com/signup**
Find us on **facebook.com/ivpbooks**
Follow us on **twitter.com/ivpbookcentre**

Inter-Varsity Press, a company limited by guarantee registered in England and Wales, number 05202650. Registered office IVP Bookcentre, Norton Street, Nottingham NG7 3HR, United Kingdom. Registered charity number 1105757.